CONTENTS

YOU HAVE OPTIONS

Your Guide to Logically Avoiding Foreclosure

By Elliott Peaks

CHAPTER 1
YOU ARE NOT ALONE

If you fall behind on your mortgage payments and fall into a pre-foreclosure status, you are not alone. There is a common belief among people in this situation that nobody could possibly know what they are going through. There can be a feeling of embarrassment and you can start blaming yourself for not taking care of your most important responsibility: keeping a roof over your head.

Common Reasons People Fall Behind On Making Mortgage Payments

Some of the common reasons that people fall behind on their mortgage payments include, but are not limited to:

- Reduction in Income
- Medical Bills
- Unexpected Increase in Expenses
- Divorce
- Death in the family
- Legal Issues

These are all examples of hardship situations that could lead to pre-foreclosure. Hardships can either be temporary or permanent. Believe it or not, even in a good economy, *life happens* and thousands of people in this country fall into pre-foreclosure every day.

CHAPTER 2
THE FIVE STAGES OF GRIEF

Pride of homeownership is a real thing. Facing the stress of losing, possibly, the largest asset that you have ever purchased can be traumatic. Homeowners in pre-foreclosure situations often experience the five stages of grief. The five stages of grief are *denial*, *anger*, *bargaining*, *depression* and *acceptance*. Everyone is different and different people go through the five stages of grief in different ways. The five stages don't necessarily occur in any specific order. And it is not uncommon for the stages to overlap. However, the goal is to ultimately reach *acceptance*. In pre-foreclosure, *acceptance* looks like acknowledging your situation, taking responsibility and committing to do something about it. 50-80% of people in pre-foreclosure situations don't do anything about it. At the end of the day, it is about protecting your financial profile, and setting your family up for success in the future.

Denial
A common theme among many homeowners in pre-foreclosure is refusing to acknowledge that they are actually in an adverse situation. It is common to not want to open your mail, to avoid answering the phone, and to refuse to seek assistance. Denial is equivalent to hiding from the problem. Denial is a way of only allowing yourself to acknowledge feelings that you can handle. Denial is a way to help you pace your feelings of grief.

Anger

4

Many homeowners begin to feel angry after they start to accept the situation they are in. It is common for people to point the finger, start to regret some of the decisions they have made and lash out at other people. The problem with anger is that it does not allow you to rationally approach the situation and work towards a solution. The longer you wait to address the situation, the worse it will become.

Bargaining

Bargaining is the stage of grief that includes desperation and regret. Many homeowners in this stage of grief will feel like they should do *anything* to save their home. This is a stage of grief where many homeowners are scammed. They explore avenues that they normally would not consider. The only thing that you should ever pay for up front in this situation is a Chapter 13 Bankruptcy, but only under certain circumstances. I will further explain in chapter 5. Anything else that you pay for up front will cost money that should be saved for the mortgage.

Depression

Many homeowners in pre-foreclosure get to a point where they lose all hope. They have tried everything and they feel as if there is nothing they can do. It is common for homeowners in pre-foreclosure to fall into depression. They think that this is the end of the world. I assure you that pre-foreclosure is never the end of the world. You have options.

Acceptance

Accepting your situation for what it is and facing reality logically will allow you to rationally explore these options. It is important to not let your emotions get the best of you. Your home in any form represents an investment in your family's future. It is important to look at that investment from a logical standpoint and weigh your options rationally.

CHAPTER 3
THE CALIFORNIA FORECLOSURE TIMELINE

It is important to familiarize yourself with the laws of your specific state. You should hire a licensed real estate professional that is familiar with your state's foreclosure timeline. Below is an example of California's residential real estate foreclosure timeline.

Day 1 – You miss a mortgage payment.

Day 30 – Your lender reports the missed payment to the credit bureaus

Day 90 – Lender issues a *Notice of Default*. A *Notice of Default* is public record and once one is issued, you are officially in pre-foreclosure.

Day 180 – Lender issues a Notice of *Trustee Sale* and you officially receive a foreclosure sale date. This sale date is also public record.

As soon as Day 201 – Your home is sold at a foreclosure auction.

If your home is sold at auction, you generally have 3 days to vacate the premises before the sheriff comes and forcefully evicts you. In addition to that, the foreclosure could potentially be on your credit report for 7 years. Foreclosure is the last thing anyone in this situation should ever want to happen. It is traumatic and financially devastating.

CHAPTER 4
YOU HAVE OPTIONS

In every pre-foreclosure situation, every homeowner has at least one of four options. I will touch on each one of these options in this chapter, and describe each option in depth in the subsequent chapters of this book. I highly advise anyone in a pre-foreclosure situation to hire a licensed real estate professional with experience working with homeowners in distressed situations. This real estate professional should be able to methodically assist you through weighing these options. These options include *loan modification, reinstatement, Chapter 13 bankruptcy and liquidation.*

Loan Modification

Loan modification is a restructuring of your existing loan by your lender. Different lenders have different loan modification programs and qualifications. It is important to keep an open line of communication with your lender. If you fall behind on your payments, you should contact your lender and ask if they have options for loan modification. A licensed real estate professional with experience in pre-foreclosures could also contact your lender as a third party and assist you in negotiating your modification for you. Loan modifications are for homeowners who have been through a temporary hardship that has caused them to fall behind, but are now able to make their payments moving forward.

Reinstatement

Reinstatement is repaying the lender in full for what you currently owe them. The first step to reinstatement when you are in pre-foreclosure is contacting your lender and ordering a reinstatement quote. That reinstatement quote will include the exact dollar amount you owe the lender including any foreclosure court and attorney fees. The quote will also include payment instructions. It is important to send the exact amount that you owe, exactly how they tell you to send it.

Chapter 13 Bankruptcy

Chapter 13 Bankruptcy is a structured repayment of your debt through a bankruptcy court. With the assistance of the court, you repay the past due balance to your lender in equal monthly payments over the course of 3-5 years. As long as you are active in the Chapter 13 Bankruptcy, you lender cannot legally foreclose on your home. This is often a costly process and you should always seek an attorney for assistance with this process. Your real estate professional should know a bankruptcy attorney that is accustomed to working with homeowners in pre-foreclosure situations.

Liquidation

Sometimes, selling your home, walking away and getting a fresh start without the burden of pre-foreclosure on your shoulders are the best things to do. If you owe more to your lender than what your house will sell for, you can do what is called a short sale. It is important to hire a licensed real estate professional that is experienced in negotiating with your lender and conducting a short sale. The lender will have to be convinced to forgive the amount above what your house is worth. If your house is worth more than what you owe, you can sell the home and use the equity to assist in your fresh start.

When going over your options, it is important to think rationally and make a decision that will benefit your life and your family. It is the best way to preserve everyone's financial and emotional well-being. I over-emphasize that you should seek the professional opinion of a licensed real estate professional who is well-versed in assisting homeowners through pre-foreclosure situations.

CHAPTER 5
OPTION 1:
LOAN MODIFICATION

Contact Your Lender

The first thing that you should do if you find yourself in pre-foreclosure is contacting your lender. You want to keep an open line of communication. The first thing that you want to ask you lender is if there are any workout options. At this time, the lender will most likely offer you the opportunity to apply for a *loan modification.* It is important during this process to not become too frustrated or angry with your lender. You want to be able to work with them towards a solution. It is a good idea to seek a licensed real estate professional that has experience communicating with banks. You can authorize the real estate professional as a third party on your account to communicate on your behalf.

What is a loan modification?

A *loan modification* is a restructuring of your existing loan by your lender. In an ideal situation, a successful loan modification can result in deferment of your past due balance, lowering of your interest rate, extension of your term, and lower payment. It is ultimately up to the investor that owns your loan and the lender's underwriting department as to whether you approved for a loan modification.

What a Lender/Investor Looks for In a Loan Modification Application

Income

The first thing that a lender will look for in a loan modification is your income. The lender wants to know if you, the borrower, have enough monthly income to comfortable cover the monthly payments. If you are a W2 employee, the lender will most likely ask for pay stubs. If you are 1099 self-employed individual, the lender will most likely ask for a 3-month recent profit and loss statement. If you own rental properties, the lender will often ask for lease agreements. The lender will always want to cross-reference your tax returns and bank statements, whether they are business tax returns and bank statements or personal tax returns and bank statements. Some lenders will allow you to include the income of a non-borrower contributor on your loan modification. A non-borrower contributor is someone who is not on the mortgage loan, but lives in the house and contributes to the household, financially. The lender will factor the total household income and mortgage payment into a front-end debt-to-income ratio (DTI). The front-end DTI is the mortgage payment divided by the total gross monthly income. The rule of thumb is that most lenders like the DTI to fall in between 31%-38%. They want to know that you make at least 3 times your mortgage payment. They want to determine that you have the monthly income to comfortably make the payment moving forward.

Payment

Many lenders will look at a loan and determine whether they can lower the payment. From the lender's perspective, if the borrower was not able to make the current monthly payment, it must be too high. They will look at the interest rate and see if they can lower it to the market interest rate. They will look at the term and see if they can extend it, sometimes to 40 years. In some cases, they may re-amortize the loan over 30 years to lower the payment. Some lenders will deny a loan modification application if there is no possible way to lower the payment.

Net Present Value

Another factor that many lenders take into consideration when looking at a loan modification application is the amount of equity in the house. They form their opinion of the value of the home. They, then, subtract the remaining loan balance from that value to determine the equity in the home. Some lenders will send a licensed BPO (Broker's Price Opinion) Agent out to the home to determine the value. Some lenders just use comparable sales in the area to form an initial opinion of value. Many lenders will deny a loan modification application if there is a significant amount of equity in the home. Lenders know that if they foreclose on a home with a lot of equity, they will get all of their money back. This is their main concern. Lenders also figure that homeowners in financial distress with a lot of equity have the option to liquidate and tap into that equity to remedy the situation.

Hardship

The last factor in a loan modification is your specific hardship. In chapter 1, I touched on some of the common reasons that people fall behind on their mortgage payments. The lender is almost certainly going to want a written explanation as to why you fell behind in the first place. Within that explanation, the lender is going to want to know that the hardship was temporary and that you now have the ability to make your mortgage payments moving forward. If you are experiencing a permanent hardship that has made it impossible for you to comfortably make your payments, it is highly unlikely that you would be approved for a loan modification. I encourage you to include every detail of your situation in your hardship letter. It can all influence the lender's decision.

When submitting a loan modification application, it is important to include the complete version of every document that they ask for. Most of the time, the lender will require that you fax the documentation and the completed application form in to the lender's loss mitigation department. It is also important to follow up with the lender via telephone consistently to ensure that your application or any of your documents don't get lost in the shuffle. This would delay the decision process. It is a good idea to find a licensed real estate professional that has experience putting together complete loan modification applications to assist you.

The Difference Between Loan Modification and Refinancing

A common misconception is that a loan modification is the same as refinancing your loan. They are completely different. A loan modification is a restructuring of your existing mortgage loan. Refinancing is taking out a new mortgage loan to pay off your existing mortgage loan. In order to qualify for a refinance, many lenders will want to see a history of on-time payments. It would also be tough to qualify with recent foreclosure history on the property. There are lending regulations that will not allow lenders to lend on a house in pre-foreclosure status. When attempting to refinance, a lender will also take your credit into account. In a loan modification application, the lender only takes income into account. If you have questions about specific qualifications for refinancing, you should contact a mortgage broker. Your licensed real estate professional should know a mortgage broker that can assist you.

CHAPTER 6
OPTION 2: REINSTATEMENT

Reinstatement is simply repaying your lender for the past due amount owed plus any attorney and legal fees from the foreclosure court.

You Must Repay Your Lender in *FULL*

The first step in reinstating your loan is to contact your lender and order a reinstatement quote. This quote will include all fees owed. The quote will include payment instructions. Generally, the fastest way to send the money is via wire transfer. The reinstatement quote will include all wire-transfer instructions. It is important that you pay the exact amount listed on the reinstatement quote before the quote expires. Reinstatement quotes are usually good for 30 days or up until your foreclosure sale date; whichever comes first.

The Lender Will Not Accept Partial Payment at This Point

Once your loan enters into pre-foreclosure status, you will not be able to pay your lender anything less than the full amount that you owe them. If you send partial payment, the lender will receive the payment, hold on to it for up to 90 days, then send it back to you, never applying it to your account.

Be Careful About Borrowing Money to Reinstate Your Loan

Be very careful about borrowing money to reinstate your mortgage loan. Only borrow the money if you have a solid plan to pay it back. If you "Rob Peter to Pay Paul," you can perpetuate a bad situation. It can ruin relationships and put you deeper into a financial hole. If you plan to reinstate, but you do not have the money, think about any assets that you can possibly liquidate or sell before you borrow the money.

CHAPTER 7
OPTION 3:
CHAPTER 13 BANKRUPTCY

Structured Repayment of Debt

Chapter 13 Bankruptcy is a repayment of debt, with the assistance of a bankruptcy court over the course of 3-5 years. This debt will include your past due balance owed to your lender, along with any other debt that you choose to include. The payments are made in equal monthly increments. The payments include all attorney and bankruptcy court fees. There is also a filing fee to begin the process. Keep in mind, that this can be a costly legal process and should be viewed as a last resort within your efforts to keep your home. As long as you are active in the Chapter 13 Bankruptcy process, your lender cannot legally foreclose. The bankruptcy court provides protection from foreclosure in the form of what is called an automatic stay. At the conclusion of the Chapter 13 Bankruptcy process, your debt is repaid and you are no longer in foreclosure.

You Must Make All of Your Payments

It is vital in a Chapter 13 Bankruptcy to make all of your payments to the bankruptcy court in full and on time. It is also important to pay your lender your regular mortgage payment in full and on time. If you fall behind on your mortgage payments while you are in a Chapter 13 Bankruptcy, your lender can file a motion to remove your automatic stay. The bankruptcy court will always approve this motion 100% of the time, and the foreclosure proceedings will pick up right where they left off. It is important to keep in mind that once in an active Chapter 13 Bankruptcy, foreclosure proceedings are only put on hold; they do not start over. The house will not be removed from pre-foreclosure until the conclusion of the Chapter 13 Bankruptcy. If the Bankruptcy is dismissed or discharged for any reason, foreclosure proceedings can also pick right back up. The bankruptcy court will also look at your income and your financial profile to determine if you are able to make the payments. It is possible that bankruptcy is not an option if the court does not feel like you have the ability to repay your debt.

Seek a Bankruptcy Attorney

Bankruptcy is a legal process and you cannot afford to make a mistake. Your financial well-being and your largest asset are on the line. Hire a professional to assist you. Your licensed real estate professional should know a good bankruptcy attorney that he or she can refer to you. It is also very important to make sure that you show up to every meeting, hearing and court date on time. If you miss one court date or if you are late, it is very possible that your bankruptcy will immediately be dismissed.

CHAPTER 8
OPTION 4: LIQUIDATION

Sometimes, the best decision you can make for you and your family is to fight the emotional attachment to the home, sell the house and move on with a fresh start and a weight lifted from your shoulders. As a homeowner, you always have the option to sell your home. However, it is important to weigh your options as soon as possible, so that you have enough time to sell your home before your foreclosure sale date arrives.

Standard Sale

If you have equity in your home, meaning your home's value is more than your total loan balance; you can sell your house and walk away with the equity in cash (minus realtor commission and closing costs). Sometimes it can be beneficial to take your equity out of your current asset with plans to move it into another asset in the near future. This is especially true if you are in a mortgage loan that you cannot afford, or a loan with an adjustable interest rate. In a standard sale situation, time is of the essence. It is important to choose a licensed real estate professional with experience dealing with pre-foreclosure situations to help you sell the home in a timely manner.

Short Sale

If your total loan balance is higher than what your home is worth, you have negative equity. At this point, your home has become a financial liability. It could take many years to get out of a negative equity position. You do not want to continue to make monthly payments with *hopes* of breaking even one day. If you want to sell your house in this situation, you want to conduct a short sale. The short sale process is a negotiation process with your bank that ultimately allows your to sell your house and forgives your for the deficient amount that is owed. Be sure to check your state's specific deficiency laws. It is important to seek a licensed real estate professional that has experience negotiating with the bank. This negotiation process can take anywhere from 3-9 months. During this time, the bank will be trying to prove their opinion of the value of the home. The negotiation concludes with a sales price that the bank agrees upon. During this process, all foreclosure proceedings will be placed on hold. It is vital during the short sale process to save money for any moving expenses. The lender will sometimes provide relocation money, but this is never a guarantee.

The Value of Your Home

At the end of the day, the value of your home is an opinion. Your home is worth what a potential buyer is willing to pay for it, based on the current market. The value of all condos, single-family homes, and residential multi-family buildings (2-4 units) is almost universally determined by taking into account all comparable sales in the area. Any deferred maintenance, especially in the major systems of the home: roof, foundation, electrical and plumbing systems, diminishes the home's value. It is always a good idea to seek a licensed real estate professional or an appraiser to give you a professional opinion on the value of your home.

CHAPTER 9
HOW TO CHOOSE YOUR REAL ESTATE PROFESSIONAL

You Can Seek Help

The thought of losing your home to foreclosure can be a scary feeling. Many people in this situation do not trust anyone and try to remedy the situation on their own. You can and should seek help in this situation. A licensed real estate professional is your best option. An ethical, experienced agent will not charge you for home retention up front. A good real estate professional will value his or her relationship with you over the compensation. If you ultimately choose to sell your home, the real estate professional will be paid in the form of commission at the close of the transaction. If you are able to avoid foreclosure and keep your home, the real estate professional will be in a position to help other people you know in the same situation. Real estate is a relationship-driven business and a good real estate professional will value his or her reputation and relationships. A good licensed real estate professional with experience dealing with pre-foreclosure situations will ensure that your home does not go into foreclosure.

Your Realtor Should Have Experience

Distressed real estate is a very specific sector of the real estate industry, with additional laws, procedures and regulations. You want to choose a licensed real estate professional that has experience dealing with pre-foreclosure situations. Your average real estate agent will not necessarily have experience within this specialized sector of the real estate industry. You should work with a real estate professional that can professionally and logically walk you through every option available to you. You also want him or her to be able to provide a professional opinion on what option is best for your specific situation. You want a real estate professional that is experienced with successfully negotiating with mortgage lenders either in a loan modification or short sale situation.

Your Realtor Should Have Connections

There are a few key people that your licensed real estate professional should have working relationships with. Your real estate professional should know a good bankruptcy attorney that is accustomed to working with homeowners in pre-foreclosure situations. Your real estate professional should know a good mortgage broker; in the event that you or someone you know is eligible for refinancing. Your real estate professional should have relationships with landlords and property management companies; in the event that you need help relocating after the liquidation of your property. A real estate professional with the right connections will allow you to logically explore all of your options.

Things an Experience, Ethical, Connected Real Estate Professional Can Do For You

A good licensed real estate professional can provide a myriad of services for you, most free of charge:

➢ The real estate professional can assist you in assembling a complete loan modification application, and sending it to your bank.
➢ The real estate professional can instruct you on the proper way to reinstate your loan and assist you in ordering your reinstatement quote.
➢ The real estate professional can refer you to a good bankruptcy attorney that can properly walk you through a Chapter 13 Bankruptcy.
➢ The real estate professional can help you sell your home and relocate in order to get a fresh start and avoid foreclosure.

If you would like to set up a free consultation with a licensed real estate professional that is experienced in dealing with pre-foreclosure situations, please call (323) 284-6533 to schedule a free initial consultation. Remember, You Have Options!

www.ingramcontent.com/pod-product-compliance
Lightning Source LLC
Chambersburg PA
CBHW031942170526
45157CB00008B/3284